Joe Acaba

Colleen Hord

Educational Media

rourkeeducationalmedia.com

Teacher Notes available at
rem4teachers.com

www.rourkeeducationalmedia.com

PHOTO CREDITS: Title page, pages 4 - 6, 14 - 17, 20, 21: © NASA; page 7, 10: © red_frog; pages 9 & 19: © Wikipedia; page 10: © prill; page 11: © Brian Scantlebury; page 13: © Orlando Sentinel; page 18: © Yuriy Kirsanov

Edited by: Precious McKenzie

Cover and interior design by: Renee Brady

Library of Congress PCN Data

Joe Acaba / Colleen Hord (Little World Biographies)
ISBN 978-1-61810-151-8 (hard cover)(alk. paper)
ISBN 978-1-61810-284-3 (soft cover)
ISBN 978-1-61810-408-3 (e-Book)
Library of Congress Control Number: 2011945877

Rourke Educational Media
Printed in the United States of America,
North Mankato, Minnesota

rourkeeducationalmedia.com

customerservice@rourkeeducationalmedia.com • PO Box 643328 Vero Beach, Florida 32964

Table of Contents

3-2-1, Blast Off!

Have you ever thought about blasting off
into outer space?

When Joe Acaba was a young boy, his father showed him movies of astronaut **Neil Armstrong** walking on the Moon.

Those movies led Joe to dream about what it would be like to go into space.

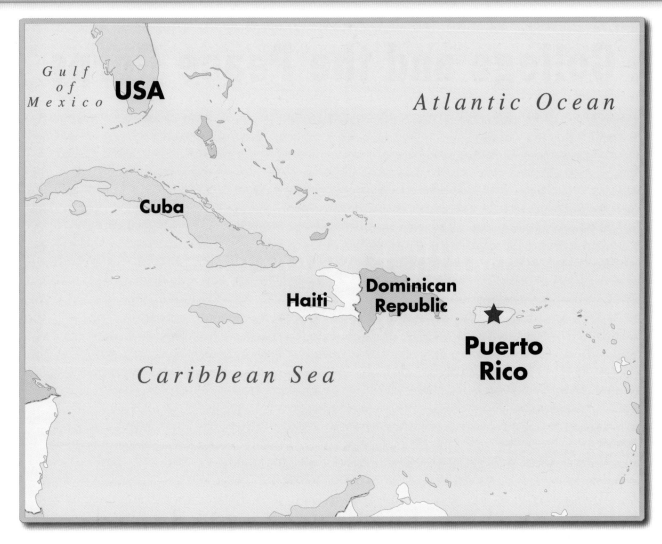

Joe's father, who moved from **Puerto Rico** to California as a child, taught Joe the importance of being a good student.

College and the Peace Corps

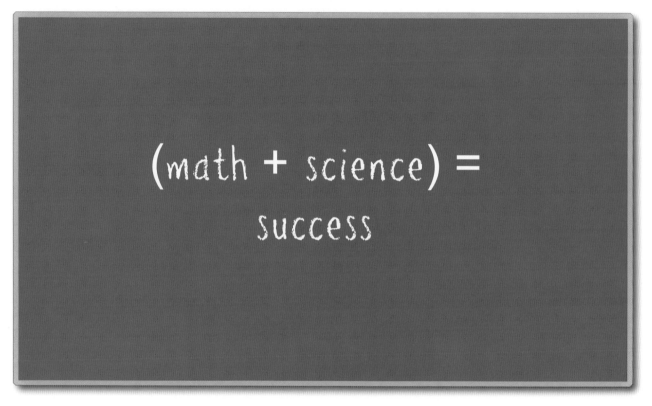

(math + science) = success

Joe remembered his father's words and always did his best in school. Joe loved to read, especially science fiction. He also liked studying math and science.

In college, Joe studied **geology**. Geology is the study of the Earth's layers of soil and rock. After college, Joe joined the Peace Corps and went to the **Dominican Republic**.

Joe taught teachers in the Dominican Republic how to teach others about taking care of the environment.

Joe spent two years in the Peace Corps as an Environmental Education Awareness Promoter. He also was the manager of the Caribbean Marine Research Center.

It was during this time Joe realized how much he liked teaching.

Teacher Astronaut

When Joe moved back to the United States, he started teaching science and math at a junior high and high school. Joe did not forget his boyhood dream of being an astronaut.

Dunnellon Middle School celebrated Joe Acaba's return to Earth and his participation in NASA's Educator Astronaut program.

In 2004, he applied to **NASA** to become a teacher astronaut.

Many teachers wanted to be in the special NASA program. Once again, Joe's hard work and studying paid off. NASA chose him for their program.

Space Shuttle Discovery

In 2009, Joe went into space on the Space Shuttle Discovery. His job was to place solar equipment on the International Space Station.

March 23, 2009 — Astronauts Joseph Acaba and Richard Arnold, worked on the robotic arm of the space shuttle while in space.

Astronauts must maintain and repair equipment on the International Space Station.

Joe's family was very proud. He was the first astronaut of Puerto Rican **heritage** to go into space.

Even though Joe is now an astronaut, he continues to teach young people everywhere he goes.

When Joe went into space, he carried a
Puerto Rican flag and a Peace Corps flag
with him. Joe requested that a Puerto Rican
folk song be played to wake him up on the
fifth morning of the space mission.

Follow Your Dreams

He tells children to get a good education and to follow their dreams, just like his father taught him to do.

Timeline

1967	Joe born (May 17)
1990	Bachelor's degree in Geology from University of California, Santa Barbara
1992	Master's degree in Geology from the University of Arizona
1999	Taught at Melbourne High School in Florida
2000-04	Taught at Dunnellon Middle School in Florida Accepted into the astronaut program
2006	Finished astronaut training
2009	Mission Specialist Educator on STS-119 space shuttle mission
2012	Joe completed 5 months in space and returned to Earth in September

Glossary

Dominican Republic (duh-MIN-i-kun ri-PUHB-lik): a country in the West Indies

geology (jee-OL-uh-jee): the study of the Earth's layers of soil and rock

heritage (HER-uh-tij): traditions that are handed down from generation to generation

NASA (na-SAH): abbreviation for National Aeronautics and Space Administration

Neil Armstrong (neel ARM-strong): the first astronaut to walk on the Moon in 1969

Puerto Rico (por-TUH re-KO): an island in the West Indies in union with the United States

Index

Websites

www.kennedyspacecenter.com

www.nasa.gov

www.spaceplace.nasa.gov

About the Author

Colleen Hord is an elementary teacher. Her favorite part of her teaching day is Writer's Workshop. She enjoys kayaking, camping, walking on the beach, and reading in her hammock.

Ask The Author!
www.rem4students.com